Y0-BGH-194

Frolicky Foot Free

Author: Jessica A. Barnum
Illustrator: Grace L. Barnum
Publisher: Lulu Press, Inc.

Text copyright© 2020 by Jessica A. Barnum
Illustrations copyright © 2020 by Grace L. Barnum
All rights reserved.

Summary: "Frolicky Foot Free" is a poem about a cardinal that experiences a pause-point-life-snag right in the midst of her frolicky flow. This story is inspired by how my Aunt Grace is enduring the aftermath intricacies of a stroke. She chose the cardinal as our "bird with a word to be heard." As the matriarch of our family, Grace's journey of fear, faith, hope, resilience, patience, perseverance, forgiveness, humor, connection and grace has "graced" us with the depths of what human being means when love and wisdom radiate our pause-point-life-snags. All of these themes have empowered her, and the spirit of her frolicky flow has not wavered. Both on the shores and in the surf of this flow she is discovering the artful dance of drawing and painting. We invite you to embrace the pause-point-life-snags that present themselves in your life too, and flutter-putter-utter through our book in your own frolicky flow. We hope this book will bring breaths of fresh air to your experiences past, present and future. Note the tetrameter (pulse of four) rhythm when reading the poem. Flap your wings and feel the beat gracing!

ISBN #: 978-1-71684-065-4

Printed by Lulu Press, Inc. in the United States of America

First Edition

Visit our website!
https://frolickyfootfree.wixsite.com/grace

Visit our Facebook page!
https://www.facebook.com/Frolicky-Foot-Free-113765857092083

Dedicated to our ancestors, cardinals and all living beings around the globe!

Donations will be made from the book sales to:

St. James Episcopal Church
76 Federal St.
New London, CT
http://www.stjamesnl.org/

Companeros de Ecuador
https://www.facebook.com/CompanerosDeEcuador/

A note from Grace: St. James is not only a place where everyone is welcome and cared for, but is also deep in its community in many ways -- a true spiritual home. The first summer trip to Ecuador was held in 2007 and comprised of folks from several Episcopal churches plus other friends from the area. Grace has been blessed to participate in all 18 summer and winter trips. Ages have ranged from twelve to eighty years old. Any and all skill levels are welcome. Letting go and going with the flow is always an important experience. The friendships made with the Ecuadorian friends are deep and treasured. The next trip has been talked about for 2022. Scholarships are provided as possible.

Sunlit blues, purples and reds,
Birds puttering in wild berry beds.

Vine to vine, wings fluttering in flight,
Beaks uttering ditties in delight.

Fluttering frozen, a frolicky foot chosen,
A sassy snag, flying to lag.

Tangling in a swirly twirly vine,
Fretful and fruitless, trying to untwine.

A tottering, tweedling, squirming bird,
Fire of spirit blazed and stirred.

Awaiting a sign, a song or a rhyme,
Stillness of time …
And silence, no chirp or chime.

Sun settling on horizon's glade,
Moon nestling on evening's shade.

A wiggling foot and a jiggling vine,
Startled and stumped in the chill of night.

Weepy eyes and sleepy wings,
Wondering what darkness brings.

The vigilance of stars dotting sky's expanse,
Earthly sounds propelling prayers to prance.

Endurance of wiggling and jiggling galore,
Soaring faith on halo's shore.

Whispering chirps to the wildness of waiting,
"Being stuck is irritating!"

Witty and wise in wily pursuit,
Tenacious will taking root.

Hopping, hoping, no pause to ponder,
Bound in courage for wilderness yonder.

Then in the fiery solace of breathing,
Love's rhapsody softening grieving,
Thickets rustling brawn and believing.

Crickets chirruping a cheery trace,
Branches extending to embrace,
Roots granting a tender pace,
The forest chanting a tale to brace,
"Go with grace ..."

A wiggling foot and a jiggling vine,
This time to intertwine,
With a saintly sign, a soul to align.

Tuning tall,
Tweeting a call,
Of love for the vine,
With moonlit shine.

Jitters dwindling,
Grit rekindling,
Beholding grace,
Emboldening the place,
Where a bird sings,
And spreads her wings.

Pulsing in the presence of her story,
Aspiring heart to fly forth shortly.

Moon settling on horizon's shade,
Sun nestling on dawn's glade.

Light splintering the gloom of gray,
A fluttering frenzy awakening the day,
Flocks of birds arriving this way,
Ignoring berries, no time for play,
Flapping feathers with this to say,
"Swirly twirly vine, away away!"

Birds swoop-swinging,
Beaks clutch-clinging,
Stubborn vine wringing,
Stuck bird singing,
"May this vine go slinging!"

Birds robustly singing,
Beaks justly clinging,
Stubborn vine releasing its clasp,
Stuck bird heaving a grateful gasp,
"It's life I grasp! May I fly at last!"

Frolicky foot f-r-e-e-i-n-g in flow,
Stubborn vine agreeing to forgo,
" 'Tis time to ebb and fall to earth's floor ..."

So goes the bird flying to explore,
Onward journey of yearning and yore.

Sunrays sailing in sync with song,
Unstuck bird gracing along ...

Frolicky Foot Free Thinking!

Dear Readers,

We had a lot of fun being creative together when making our book. Creativity is wondrous, and we invite you to reflect on and explore your own creativity. Think about how you like to be creative in various art forms. Being an "artist" is being creative in any way you'd like. Do you like to draw, paint, write, sculpt with clay-wood-metal, dance, sew, sing, play an instrument, arrange flowers in vases and gardens, make jewelry and perhaps blend art forms together? What other art forms can you think of? Just like we shared Aunt Grace's experience with a stroke as a cardinal in a poem with vibrant illustrations, perhaps you'd like to ponder the prompts below and create the art forms of your choosing. Spark your artful self and have fun in your frolicky flow!

Our questions are based on the themes that are present in our book. And, we encourage you to think of other themes and ideas you detected and create art based on them too! YOU are the artist of your own creativity, so go for it!

Have you ever felt fear? Did you embrace it or escape it? What is the story? Choose an art form and create what fear is to you.

Have you ever had faith in a situation, an idea, in yourself or someone else? What is the story? Choose an art form and create what faith is to you.

Have you ever started a thought with, "I hope ..."? What is the story? Choose an art form and create what hope is to you.

After you've been through a challenging situation, have you ever experienced resilience? Perhaps you had a thought such as, "I made it through the challenge, I've bounced back and I'm stronger and wiser than ever." What is the story? Choose an art form and create what resilience is to you.

Has patience ever helped you get through a situation when you felt frustrated, confused or scared? What is the story? Choose an art form and create what patience is to you.

Have you ever been stuck and perseverance helped you become unstuck? Perhaps you were stuck in a situation, on a thought in your mind or with your body, and you persevered with determination and motivation. What is the story? Choose an art form and create what perseverance is to you.

Have you ever experienced forgiveness when something happened to you? Perhaps at first you blamed the situation, yourself or someone else and then you decided to forgive. What is the story? Choose an art form and create what forgiveness is to you.

Humor! Have you ever been in a serious situation when you felt the world caving in on you, and then humor stepped in and the lightness of laughter helped ease your head and heart? What is the story? Choose an art form and create what humor is to you.

What do you connect to within yourself and with the world? How do you enrich those connections? Connection is like creativity; it comes in many forms. Think about the power of connection and how and why it thrives inside of yourself as well as between you and other people, animals, nature, communities and other examples you think of. What is the story? Choose an art form and create what connection is to you.

What does grace ~ graceful ~ gracious mean to you? When have you experienced any of these? What is the story? Choose an art form and create what grace ~ graceful ~ gracious is to you.

Have you ever seen a cardinal? How did it act? Did it sound like it was saying, "I'm red, red, red, red, red"? What is the story? Cardinal males are bright red and females are tan with an orange beak. They symbolize love, devotion, good fortune and a connection to our loved ones in our past, present and future. Choose an art form and create what a cardinal means to you.

With artful love for YOU,

Jessica and Grace

Author
Jessica A. Barnum

Jessica (Jessie B., Ms. Jess) has loved teaching English & Reading, yoga and biking to her students over the years, in both Vermont and Colorado. She loves writing poetry, plays & stories, biking of all sorts, hiking, skiing & snowboarding, yoga, Reiki, gardening, cooking and exploring new sites. It is her livelihood to adventure and blossom in this world with her husband and his children, family, friends, colleagues and her former and current students. She dearly loves the people in her life, and finds it magical how the spirituality and love that radiates from connection breathes abundantly and eternally. Her inspiration for writing comes from playful, reflective time with nature, literature of all sorts, dreams, intuitive stirrings, observations of animals and people's experiences and stories. You will often find Jessica on a bicycle, hugging trees or talking to deer and birds, especially owls lit up by the full moon.

Illustrator
Grace L. Barnum

Grace worked with young children and families addressing autism after a career in business. Having been educated at Syracuse University and graduating from Stone College prepared her for the business world, yet Grace learned that working with kids was her preference. As a mother of a daughter and a son and a grandmother of four, all they have brought to her helped her realize the gift of working with children. Most decidedly, Grace is a typical grandmother completely devoted to her four grandchildren and her self-proclaimed awesome family no matter what. She spent many years with her Portuguese Water Dogs. She states that one was a rascal and one very sweet. In her spare time, she embarked on many trips to her beloved Ecuador and still has dear friends there. Much time has been devoted to St. James Episcopal Church where she lives out her deepening spiritual life.

~ Aunt Grace and her niece Jessica in Montana in 2004! ~